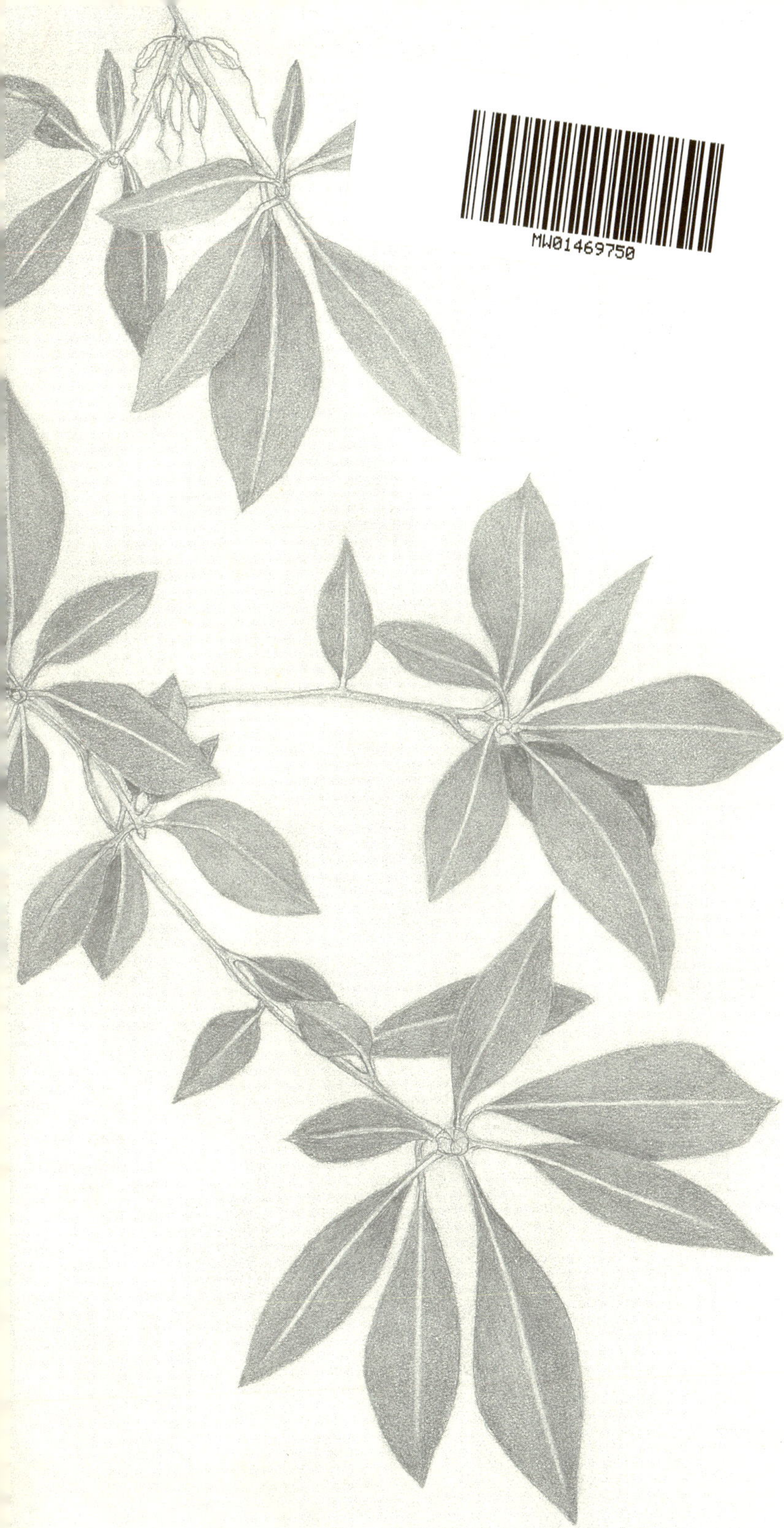

Hilltop
My Story

Starbush
Illicium floridanum

Native azalea
Rhododendron canescens

Hilltop
My Story

EMORY SMITH

DRAWINGS BY JUNE GONCE

FRIENDS OF HILLTOP ARBORETUM
Baton Rouge, Louisiana

Copyright © 1995 by Friends of Hilltop Arboretum, Inc.

Drawings copyright © 1995 by June Gonce

Manufactured in the United States of America
All rights reserved

First printing
04 03 02 01 00 99 98 97 96 95   5 4 3 2 1

Designer: Amanda McDonald Key
Typeface: Sabon
Printer and binder: Thomson–Shore, Inc.

ISBN 0-9649-6920-3

The paper in this book meets the guidelines for permanence and durability of the Committee on Production Guidelines for Book Longevity of the Library Resources Council. ∞

To my wife, Annette
(original dedication of *Hilltop*)

Contents

Original Foreword to *Hilltop* / ix

Preface / xi

Hilltop: My Story / 1

Dedication of Hilltop Arboretum / 59

Appendix: Emory Smith's Favorite Plants / 63

Original Foreword to
Hilltop

This little book is a beautiful expression of a philosophy of life that has produced a wonderful living environment—one that for many years has produced great enjoyment not only for its owners, but also for the entire community and many LSU students.

If you were privileged to enter the Smiths' living room, you undoubtedly would gasp at the view from the picture window and would realize why no suggestions ever were made by the landscape architect. Emory and Annette have set their modest residence in the midst of an already gorgeous natural landscape and then have very sensitively guided nature to perfection.

> Robert S. Reich, Director
> School of Landscape Architecuture
> Louisiana State University
> Baton Rouge
> 1977

Preface

Lionel Emory Smith was born on August 22, 1891, in Dallas County, Iowa. He was the second child and older son of Horace Greeley Smith and Viretta Pierce. He married Annette Gourley in 1915. The couple moved to Baton Rouge in 1918. They had two daughters. In 1929 he purchased a twenty-acre farm, which he called Hilltop. Emory Smith worked for the Postal Service, and not until after retirement in 1950 did he develop the idea of establishing Hilltop as a sanctuary for native plants. Annette Smith died in 1980. In 1981, Emory Smith and his daughters, Esther Smith Webb and Gwendolyn Smith Patterson, donated the property to Louisiana State University. Emory Smith died at Hilltop in March, 1988, at the age of ninety-six.

Emory Smith was and is the spirit of Hilltop. To preserve his spirit is the reason this book is being published. This edition is a combination and condensation of his book *Hilltop*, written in 1977, and a later autobiography, *My Story*, written in 1982, and is being published by Friends of Hilltop Arboretum, Inc. In May, 1982, after the property had been donated to LSU, Friends of Hilltop was organized when Emory Smith asked some of his friends and neighbors to form a support group. The stated purpose of Friends of Hilltop is "to see that Hilltop becomes a complete arboretum of native Southern trees, shrubs, and wildflowers, and to encourage its free and effective use by both the University and the general public."

Friends of Hilltop wishes to thank Esther Smith Webb and Gwendolyn Smith Patterson for giving their permission to publish this edition of their father's work, and June Gonce and Elizabeth Nell Dubus for their ideas and hard work, which made this publication possible.

Hilltop
My Story

Silverbell
Halesia diptera

Oakleaf hydrangea
Hydrangea quercifolia

I WAS BORN ON A FARM IN DALLAS County, Iowa, just a mile north of DeSoto. DeSoto was a village of about four hundred people which would have had no importance at all had it not been on the Rock Island Railroad's main line between Chicago and Denver.

It was the railroad which made DeSoto an interesting place for me. Most of the trains, both passenger and freight, did not stop. I was thrilled to watch the fast passenger trains tearing through, whistle screaming, "Get out of the way." I was almost as fascinated by the mile-long freight trains where men walked on top of the fast-moving cars to man the brakes.

Some trains did stop at DeSoto. A person could get on the local train in the morning, go to Des Moines, the Iowa state capital, and come back on the local train in the evening.

Many other things were shipped by rail. Farmers took hogs and cattle they had raised to the livestock pens at the station, from which they were loaded onto freight cars and shipped to Chicago. Other freight cars were loaded with wheat, oats, or corn from the grain elevator. Today, trains no longer run on the Rock Island Railroad. DeSoto must be a much less interesting place.

The railroad ran down the level valley along Bulger Creek

where little grading was required. The one business street of the town was on top of the hill, about three blocks from the station.

On the first corner was the oldest and largest store on the street, I. Hoch and Son, which sold a variety of things, from groceries to farm machinery. The store was built on the slope of the hill, with the basement and the lot behind it used for the display of farm machinery. There was a butcher shop across the street. Dry goods and clothing could be bought from Bower Brothers.

One small but important shop was that of Frank Irvin, the tinsmith. He stocked buckets, tubs, wash boilers, and stovepipe. Some of them were factory produced, but the best he made by hand in his own shop.

The most interesting place on the business street for me was the shop of Mr. Anderson, the blacksmith. Like the character in the Longfellow poem, the smith worked under a big tree, but this one was not a chestnut tree. It was an old cottonwood, which at one season of the year spread a liberal amount of cotton over the neighboring lots.

The blacksmith was a very important person in the days before farm implements were standardized and dealers began to carry replacement parts for everything that might wear out or break. In the fall and early winter, Mr. Anderson was very busy shoeing horses. At that time, all power was, quite literally, horsepower. For winter, horses had to be shod with sharp points on their shoes to prevent them slipping on icy roads. I loved to watch Mr. Anderson at his forge and anvil. It seemed like magic the way he could make almost anything out of hot metal.

DeSoto had one small factory for the making of clay tile, most of which was used in our area for draining land that was too wet to produce good crops. Wagons hauled the clay from a pit south of town. The clay had been obtained from a pit on our farm until they dug down to a layer of limestone. The clay was dumped into a machine which mixed it with a little water to make a very stiff goo. This was forced through a die from which it came out in tubular form and was cut into twelve-inch sections. These were stacked in a shed to dry for a week or two and then placed in round kilns, where they were burned at a red heat. They went into the kiln a dull color and came out red and very hard.

DeSoto had two churches, a Methodist and a Disciples of Christ, which some Methodists, with a feeling of superiority, often called Campbellites. There was a multi-grade school in a two-story brick building. People were very proud of their village.

Our farm was on the main road north of DeSoto, eighty acres of hilly land with a few small ditches in the pasture. Several acres of pasture were covered with timber: bur oak, wild cherry, elm, hickory, and basswood, with sumac and hazel brush.

The Hemphill farm bordered ours for a half mile along one side. I called Mr. Hemphill a gentleman farmer. With more than four hundred acres of land, he was never known to do any of the work himself. He was always dressed in a neat suit, not in denim overalls like the other farmers. He ignored people he was not interested in, including all children. His land was farmed by renters who paid a share of the crop as rent. He lived in a large white house with a neat front yard with a clump of peonies in the center and with clematis and multiflora roses growing on trellises against the house. The grounds were surrounded by large old silver maples. Even the barns were different. Most Iowa barns were unpainted or painted red. Mr. Hemphill's barns were painted gray with yellow-green trim. Just past his house, he had a large orchard of fall apples, apples which would not keep for winter use. I felt both bold and fearful when I sneaked under the fence to get an apple or two to eat on the way home from school.

The Ganoe farm was across the road from our place. We could see the barn on a hill about a quarter of a mile away. I liked to watch Mr. Ganoe's flock of geese. Every morning they would come walking in single file down the hill, through the grass to the pools along the creek, just over the fence. There they would spend the morning, splashing in the water with much squawking and flapping of wings.

Three quarters of a mile north from our farm was a bridge over the South Raccoon River. The land there belonged to the Van Meters, a family that had come to the community in the early days and had bought several hundred acres along the river. The upper part of their land was hilly, much of it covered with timber: walnut, butternut, hickory, and oak.

It was here that boys hunted for walnuts in the fall and stained their hands so dark brown from hulling walnuts that it took a week for their skin to bleach out to a normal color. The woods was also a favorite for squirrel hunters. And there were sandbars along the river where the entire neighborhood got its supply of sand and gravel.

The Van Meter farm was very fertile, level, river-bottom land. It had produced crops that made the family wealthy. Another source of their wealth was the mill. Many years earlier, a dam had been built across the river and a mill had been set up to grind the local wheat into flour.

I liked the mill. I liked to hear the water falling over the dam, and to listen to the mill grinding the wheat. I liked to watch the miller, dressed in white clothes and all covered with flour-dust. I liked to see the wagons go past our place, hauling the flour to the railroad at DeSoto. A few years later, a flood on the river washed out the dam, and the mill never ran anymore.

Typically, land near the river was likely to be hilly and timbered. However, most of the better land in this part of Iowa was former prairie land, which was level, and few trees were found except for those which had been planted around the farm buildings. Most of this land was in cultivated crops.

The farms might be very different, but nearly every farmer raised corn and hogs, Iowa's No. 1 products.

Father was an exceptionally good farmer, whose income came from dairy cows, hogs, and poultry. Although he only attended college for one year, his education did not stop there. He was a great reader and would buy books on any subject that interested him. He subscribed to the leading farm papers, *Wallace's Farmer, Hoard's Dairyman, Rural New Yorker,* and others. Some of the best magazines were always in our house, including the *Literary Digest* and *Review of Reviews.*

You could feel sure of his competence as a farmer if you simply stood at the edge of the field and looked over the corn on both sides of the fence. The corn on his side was darker green, with heavier stalks, and there were none of the cockleburrs which infested the neighbors' corn.

Father had learned very early to rotate his crops, so the field in corn this year would be planted in oats next spring, and after that, in clover hay, which would add nitrogen to the soil. He did not sell his hay and grain but planned to feed it all to his livestock and then spread the manure on the fields and pastures to keep up the fertility. Father's system gave a steady income that did not fluctuate greatly, and it kept up the fertility of the soil.

There was always a good garden on the farm, an orchard, and a berry patch, with raspberries, blackberries, Juneberries, grapes and currants, and often strawberries.

To operate such a diversified farm requires a variety of machinery. Father planned to buy at least one labor-saving machine every year: a grain binder, a riding plow, a cream separator. To buy a new machine meant also to provide shelter for it, because nothing was ever left exposed to the weather. He liked to see good equipment in the house, so he bought the best kitchen range on the market, and he screened in the back porch for a summer kitchen. In time, he had the cream separator, the churn, and the washing machine, all run by a gasoline engine.

I was two and a half years old. It was the morning after my brother, Gilbert, was born. When I came downstairs, there was a strange woman in the kitchen, a Mrs. Lamkin, whom I loathed at first sight. There was a bed in the parlor where no bed had ever been before. I was told that my mother had something in bed with her which I would love to see. I would not have wanted to see it even if it had been a new puppy instead of a baby brother. I was completely unhappy and frustrated. Perhaps that is the reason that, later in the morning, the window curtain in the little downstairs bedroom was found to be on fire and the window casing was charred before the fire could be put out. I was asked if I had started the fire and I said no. Then they asked me a tricky question: "Did you get the matches in the kitchen or in the parlor?" Being a truthful boy, I answered, "In the parlor." After a few days, Mrs. Lamkin was gone and I found that my mother still loved me in spite of that new brother. My world was safe once more.

My mother was, very simply, my whole world until I was almost six years old and beginning to look forward to starting school. I knew my mother loved me, but that does not half express what she meant to me.

She was the first person I saw when I woke up in the morning, and the one who put me to sleep at night. My mother sang to me and read to me and told stories about when she was a little girl. I especially liked the scary story about the time the Indians came to her house.

Mother seldom either praised or criticized, but she gave me a feeling of approval that Father never did. Though she was not profuse in her verbal expressions of affection, if I was hurt or if anything went wrong, I went straight to her. She had the magic that made everything better, no matter what the trouble. If something exciting occurred, I always hurried to tell her, for she understood my thrill, and shared it with me.

Mother was a good cook who always remembered Father's preferences. Father liked cornbread, so it was served often. He believed in eating greens, so they were on the table from the time the first wild greens began coming up in the spring.

Mother liked to prepare special dishes for every occasion that invited it: Sunday dinners, holidays, birthdays. Birthdays were special at our table, though we never had birthday parties.

I remember those meals with pleasure. I have never since tasted the equal of her whole wheat muffins, her roast chicken stuffed with dressing, her gingerbread, her apple dumplings, or her pumpkin pie.

One of the first jobs with which I could really help my

mother was gathering the eggs. Mother had a good many hens, and some of them would try to hide their nests in strange places. It was a triumph for a small boy to find a nest of eggs out in the tall grass or back in the barn under the hay.

About the time I started school, I was called upon to help with the morning and evening chores. From gathering eggs and feeding two or three calves, I learned how to milk Juno, the big red cow who was so gentle and easy to milk. The amount of my chores increased steadily over the years until I was doing as much of the morning work as Father was.

The chores went something like this: I was usually the first one up in the morning, and in wintertime that was well before daylight. I started by building the fires, for we did not have a furnace. Then I put on my wraps and went to the barn to feed the horses and cows. Then I would get the buckets to start milking, and by that time, my oldest sister, Vida, and my younger brother, Gilbert, would be on hand to help. After we had finished milking, we took the milk to the house, where we had a DeLavel Separator which skimmed the cream from the milk. The separator was turned by hand at that time, and the work was rather strenuous. The skimmed milk was divided up to feed about a dozen small calves. When they had been fed, I could eat my breakfast, put up my noon lunch, and hurry off for the mile walk to school.

I do not think that the mile walk ever seemed difficult. We might have to hurry in the morning to get there on time, but the trip home in the evening was more leisurely. There were often a number of children going along together, and there were many things to see along the way. Where we cut across the pasture, there was a tiny stream where we might have the luck to see a green frog. There was one long stretch along the Hemphill place where the field, which was a little higher than the road, was fenced with a combination of wire and boards. If there was a winter snowstorm with the wind from the west, the snow would pile up in high drifts below that fence, and often the top would be packed hard. Then it was much better to walk on top of the snowdrift than in the road.

If one of us hit a soft place in the drift and went down waist-deep in the snow, that only added to the fun, though we always tried to pick our way so we would not break through. In the fall, there were flowers along the road, goldenrod and asters. If a farm buggy or wagon came along, we always hoped it would stop and give us a ride.

The evening chores were much the same. This work had to be done every day. There is no seasonal slack on a farm where the income is derived from dairy cows, hogs, and poultry.

Two or three times a week, a ten-gallon can of cream had to be taken to the station to be shipped to an ice-cream factory in Des Moines. It was necessary to move rather briskly to get the morning chores done and have that can of cream at the station before the local train came in at 9:45. Sometimes I had to rush to have it on the baggage truck before the train came in. We had an old buggy that rattled all over, and a horse that needed no encouragement to pick up speed. I seldom, if ever, missed, but there were times when I heard the train whistle in the distance and came down the road at such a rattling speed that everyone on the main street of town knew that it was a race, and the loafers in front of the grocery store were laying bets as to whether my old buggy or the train would get to the station first.

Then the time came when I was needed in the field, so I

was given a three-horse team and a riding plow. I liked that. There was corn to be worked, so I rode the cultivator and soon learned to manipulate the shovels with my feet so that I would scrape out almost every weed. At haying time, there was the mower to ride and I could watch the timothy fall over the sicklebar. In time, I would learn to stack hay so that it would shed water in the heaviest rain, and be proud of doing a man's work, but not yet.

Corn was the most important crop, but a considerable amount of wheat and oats was grown. Those crops were more interesting to small boys because of the excitement at harvest time. A Deere or McCormick binder was always used to harvest the grain, which was cut close to the ground and tied in bundles or sheaves that were dropped off behind the machine. Someone followed to put those bundles into a shock. About eight of them were stood up and pressed closely together. Then two of the bundles were folded over the top to shed any possible rain. The grain finished drying out in the shock, ready for the threshing. Large threshing machines, powered by steam traction engines, went from one farm to another through the community. This occasion was fun for small boys, but it was strenuous for the adults. Any threshing job required at least twelve men and six teams, and might require more if the fields were distant or if the grain were sold and hauled directly to the grain elevator.

The farm wife would be busy also, for she usually had to feed that crowd at least one meal. There was no skimping on food, for there was rivalry among the farm women as to who could put up the best meal. She asked neighbors to help her and then did her best. She was likely to serve chicken and beef or pork, vegetables from the home garden, and pie or cake or both. A dinner for the threshers was something to remember.

In the summer, I frequently had to hoe in the garden, although I did not like the job very much. Then, at the beginning of one summer vacation, it was decided that I was old enough to take over the full responsibility for the vegetable garden. I knew how to plant the seed, how to hoe out the weeds, and how to watch for hornworms on the tomato plants. But hoeing in the garden, all by myself, was boring and monotonous. The garden was out of sight of the house, and I had not reached the age to feel very great responsibility. After I had hoed awhile, I would begin to think about being thirsty and go to the well. Then I would begin to think that the raspberries might be getting ripe, and I would go over and look along the row to see if there were any ripe enough to eat. Then I discovered I could just sit in the shade of an apple tree and daydream. The garden was a moderate success, because plants will grow in spite of much neglect. There was enough that I was sure to have the garden to care for next year.

One chore I always enjoyed was bringing in the cows from the pasture. Sometimes they would not recognize that it was time for them to come in, and I would have to hunt for them out in the back woods pasture under the bur oak trees among the hazel bushes.

There were dozens of fascinating glimpses of nature on the farm which took the pain out of hard work. There were granite boulders showing above the grass in the pasture, and I was always curious about how they got there and why they were of such a variety of colors.

Along the edge of the cornfield, I would watch the play of the striped ground squirrels, but if I came close, they disappeared in a maze of holes in the ground. The ground squirrels made holes so small that you hardly saw them, but over in the meadow, the groundhog or woodchuck made a hole that was six inches across, and then heaped up the dirt in a big mound where he could sit and watch what was going on in his world.

The farm was full of wonders. My love of the woods pasture gave me a keen interest in what it contributed to our way of living. In most years, there were wild plums in the summer and hazel nuts in the fall. One tree gave great promise because of its beautiful flowers and its large crop of fruit: the crab apple. But the little apples are extremely hard and sour.

One year we did use them. Farmers have always been dependent on the weather; more so in earlier times. One year, before our berry patch was bearing, the weather did not cooperate with the farmers at all. There had been a late frost which had destroyed all the fruit buds in the orchard. Then there was such excessive rain that crops were almost a complete failure. There was no fruit at all in prospect for the winter, and no money to buy anything.

Meanwhile, across the barnyard, by the old clay pit, there was a clump of crab apple trees bending down with the weight of their fruit. Out of necessity, Father and Mother decided to experiment with the wild fruit. They had a device that would cut the core out of the crab apple, so they prepared some of the wild fruit and boiled it down in sorghum syrup. The result was a strong-flavored, chewy, preserved fruit so dark in color it was jokingly called "tar," but it had an acceptable fruit taste. My parents then preserved a quantity of crab apples in the same way. These added much to our restricted diet that winter.

That was the same year that I discovered something else about wild fruit. Among these crab apple trees by the clay pit were some hawthorn trees that bore extra-large fruit, large enough that children would enjoy eating them. Late in the winter, while playing the woods, I scraped snow and leaves from under the hawthorn trees and found the red haws as good as when they were fresh in the fall. Then I tried the crab apples. Not only were they perfectly preserved, but the freezing had reduced the sourness so much that they were highly acceptable to a boy who craved fresh fruit as much as I did.

It was the same love of trees that led to maple-syrup making. It began as nothing but a boy's stunt. We had heard of making syrup from maples, and since the trees around our house were all maples, we decided to see what the sap tasted like. It was no trouble to bore a hole in one of the trees and drive in a spout made from an elderberry stem with the pith pushed out. A fruit jar caught the sap.

Our trees were not the sugar maples normally used in syrup making, but the sap was sweet and pleasant to drink. We drank all of that first day's yield. The next day we begged Mother to let us put a kettle of sap on the kitchen stove and let it boil down into syrup. We lost interest before the boiling was completed, so Mother had to finish the job.

The result was so satisfactory that Father and Mother decided they would get ready in advance for the next year and make a quantity of the syrup for home use. The maple sap runs in early spring, after most of the snow is gone but before the ground is dry enough for spring work. Then, work on a farm is rather slack.

Father ordered metal spouts to use on the trees, and for sap buckets we prepared fruit jars with wire loops around the top. We tapped dozens of silver maples and even the big box elder tree. We used a big iron kettle over an open fire for boiling. The sap ran too fast for one kettle, so the tinsmith made a big pan to fit over four holes of the kitchen range. Since the range helped heat the house, there was always a fire in it. We found the maple syrup to be just as good as if it had been made from regular sugar maples.

I had one brother and five sisters, but the younger ones were never my playmates. My brother, Gilbert, was two and a half years younger than I. We both liked to climb the trees around our place, starting with the big willow tree right by our back door. He was a better climber than I was, but he was not persistent. I never did get over my love for climbing trees until I became too old to do it safely. We both liked to play in the little creek that flowed through the barnyard, to wade in it and to build dams which would make pools in which we could sail our improvised boats.

My sister Vida, who was two and a half years older than I, shared many of my interests. We both loved wildflowers. We liked to hunt them and to learn about them. At that time, there were no herbicides available for farm use, so there were many wildflowers to be found very close to our house.

There was a little wooded pasture across the road where we could find crab apples in bloom, and underneath the trees there were white trillium, trout lilies, and violets. Along the fence row, we could discover Solomon's seal, prairie roses, wild asters, goldenrod, and wild sunflowers. We even loved the dandelions which tried to take over our front yard, and the big-leafed burdock plants in the fence corners, which had clinging burrs that we could use to make baskets and other objects.

Vida and I both loved the birds. We were curious about their names and about where they built their nests. We were especially attracted to the little birds. That included the house wren that always built a nest in the tin can up under the edge of the porch roof, and what we called the snow birds, the juncos and chickadees that came in small flocks in wintertime to pick up the crumbs that were thrown out on the snow. There were also some little birds we called wild canaries, warblers with yellow markings who seemed to like the grassy spots along the edges of the fields.

I could not understand how the barn swallow could build a nest of mud that would hold firmly to the eaves of the barn or how the Baltimore oriole could weave a nest of grass and horsehair, a frail-looking sack as it hung on the outermost branches of the maple tree, but which would go through the worst storms undamaged.

We did not have any field guide, so our names for the birds were not always accurate. The only good colored pictures of birds that we had were the little cards that the Arm and Hammer Baking Soda Company put in the top of every package. Whenever a new package of soda was opened, Vida and I would be right there to see what bird picture it contained this time, and which of us might claim it.

I liked to read and would read almost anything. Most of the lessons at school were not really work. They were just something else to read. In high school, I found that nature is an open book for those who wish to learn. For me, high school was characterized by the influence of one man, B. M. Cobb. He loved to teach, and he could inspire young people with a desire to learn. He was the best teacher I ever had. Mr. Cobb was passionately fond of good literature. He inspired us to read it, to memorize sections of it, and to express ourselves effectively.

With my love of nature, it was the science courses—physics, botany, and physical geography—that appealed to me most. I could not do as much with physics as I wished, because I did not have a good place to work on it. For botany and physical geography, however, the whole outdoors was all the laboratory that I needed. In botany, I discovered plants on the farm I never suspected were there, and with a little study, I learned their names. Even the most familiar plants came to mean more to me as I learned about their structure and their growth patterns.

In physical geography, I learned that the granite boulders scattered here and there on our farm were left there by the great glaciers that once covered the land. The layers of limestone, so prominent in the old claypit, were formed long ago when this part of the country was under the sea. I could watch our little creek and South Raccoon River changing their courses, just as the book said they would.

Sometimes I ran into a mystery for which I could find no explanation. By the bridge over South Raccoon River there was a high bluff covered with trees and with rock ledges showing across its face. One day when I had gone to the river for a load of sand, I took the time to tie my team and climb that bluff to see what was on top of it. There, under the trees, I was surprised to find a long slab of sandstone. The amazing thing to me was that the slab was not smooth but had a pattern of wavy grooves running the length of the stone. I was sure they were not man-made. They were from some natural cause, but what that could be was more than I could guess.

Some time later, I was in Des Moines, where I visited the Iowa State Museum. There I saw a block of sandstone on display with grooves just like those I had seen on the bluff above the river. In response to my question, the attendant explained that the grooves were made by water running over loose sand, which later hardened into stone.

That sounded all right, because it was the same wavy pattern I had seen along our little sandy creek and along the margin of the river. But what had turned that sand into stone, and how did it get there on the bluff, sixty feet above the river? This suggested other mysteries I had read about that seemed to call for extremely powerful forces and immense periods of time, a little hard to fit in with the Genesis story of creation that had been taught to me. There were so many things I wanted to know.

The same father who stressed learning also inhibited it. His influence was lessened by the fact that he was hot-tempered. There were times when he seemed to lose control of himself so completely that he was not restrained by reason or by his own interests in the matter. I was afraid of my father.

His violent temper might not have affected me so much had not the same lack of restraint appeared in his religion. He seemed to have been a regular Methodist until he became involved with members of the Holiness Association and accepted their teaching. Though he claimed to be saved and sanctified, perfected in the love of God, that did not control his temper. He still had angry outbursts, but now he was convinced they were completely justified.

His religion was almost completely evangelistic. Our life here was just a preparation for death, the Judgment Day, and life after death. He liked evangelists who preached about Judgment Day and hellfire. We had family prayer every evening before going to bed, and Father read a section from the Bible. He did not pick out the comforting passages like the Twenty-third Psalm. A religion of fear: fear of my father and of his God, fear of Judgment Day, fear of death and of what might follow it.

That was the atmosphere in which I lived. The only time I was entirely free from that feeling of terror was when I forgot the problems and opinions of men to give myself to nature. I remember one occasion particularly.

We had all gone to church that Sunday morning. When the midday meal was over, I slipped out, grabbed my hat, and headed for the back woods pasture. I never had much time for the things I wanted to do. On school days, there were chores to be done that took until after dark. On Saturdays, there was usually work to fill the entire day. But, for two or three hours, this afternoon was mine, and I wanted to get away to the world of nature. The sun was shining and I was on my way to the back woods. I had often found sanctuary there, away from fear and loneliness. Sin and Hell and Eternity are church dogmas, formed by the minds of men and intended for controlling other men. They have no meaning at all in the world of nature.

The back pasture was not a large place, just a few acres, two-thirds of it covered by thick woods. As I walked down under the bur oaks, my fears and resentments began to slip away. If I wanted to hide away, the sumac thicket was so dense that no one could see in, but today I just wanted to be by myself and enjoy this little world of wonder.

There was enough to enjoy and marvel at on this late spring afternoon. Just over the fence, in the edge of the meadow, there was a dense, tangled thicket with a few larger trees in the center. Scattered in front of them were wild crab apples still showing their pink flowers, and hawthorns white with bloom. At the end of the thicket, there was a rank bed of yellow violets in full flower, and along the fence, prairie roses were sending up strong shoots and beginning to show their pink buds.

Suddenly, across the meadow, I saw a groundhog sitting bolt upright on his mound, surveying the landscape, but when I took a step forward, he gave a yelp and vanished in his hole like a flash.

Now the brush along the fence became so thick I was glad to drop back and follow a cow path bordered by head-high stunted trees and hazel bushes. Under these, I soon came to a wide spread of wild blue phlox, and on the other side of the path, near the fence, a line of larkspur, standing erect with purple flowers. A little farther on, the larkspur was mixed with graceful, nodding, red and yellow columbine. I did not pick any of the flowers. I only paused to look at them as I made my way down the path.

Around the corner of the meadow fence, there was a boggy spot where weeds and slough grass grew, where red-wing blackbirds rose with their ringing calls, flashing their bright scarlet wing patches. Here, wild strawberries were in full bloom, and a few of the berries were turning red.

By this time I was thirsty, so I headed down the hollow toward the spring. The spring was secluded and did not show itself to the world. The banks above the wide, grassy ditch were covered with oak and elm trees and hazel bushes, which not only gave concealment, but also shut out the late cold winds, so that here the white clover was blooming and the bees were hard at work.

The spring itself was a sparkling stream flowing out at the base of a low bank, clear and cold in the hottest weather. I drank. In front of the spring were little pools and boggy spots, made by the cows when they came to drink. As I looked over these pools, little green frogs jumped in every direction, but a large leopard frog continued to sit in quiet dignity until I came close, and then, with a loud "Rumph," he leaped into the weeds. I watched in fascination as a single crawfish sunned himself at the bottom of a pool while a multitude of waterbugs skimmed over its surface.

Finally I made my way down the little stream toward the lower pasture fence. At one place, water splashed over a pile of granite boulders. I had read that granite is made up of three kinds of crystals: quartz, mica, and feldspar. I guessed that it was the feldspar that gave the granite its distinctive color of red or green or gray. But I wondered what made the crystals stick together so firmly that a boulder could scarcely be broken with a sledgehammer.

Now I saw that the sun was setting. There were chores to be done before supper. It was with a feeling of inward peace that I began to look for the cows, to drive them home for the milking. I loved the trees and flowers for themselves, but at that time nature was, first of all, a haven where I could escape from tension and fear.

During all this time, Father was an active member of the Holiness Association. The leaders were aggressively trying to expand. They had set up a school at Oskaloosa, Iowa, which they called Central Holiness University. That was where I was sent for my further education, and I was so much under the spell of their religious philosophy that I approved the choice completely.

Central Holiness University was not a university, nor even an accredited college. The directors of the school were rigid fundamentalists. There was no vocational slant to their instruction except for those who were planning to be preachers. This was not a school for education, but for indoctrination into a narrow and obsolete philosophy of life. There was thorough regulation of the students' lives. Attendance at daily chapel and Sunday religious services was compulsory. Students could leave the campus only at certain times without special permission. Competitive sports were discouraged except for tennis, and there was only one tennis court. Football was absolutely forbidden. Dating was permitted on Saturday evening, but only in the parlor, under the watchful eye of the matron.

Most of the students were from Holiness Association families, so it would have been natural to assume that they already had the religious experience that the association preached. That assumption was not made. When I came to the school, I soon found that although classes were required, religious meetings were far more important. At the testimony and prayer meetings, students were encouraged to report on the state of their religious experience. These meetings were often dominated by a spirit of unthinking emotionalism. I tried to participate, but I could not fit into the spirit very well. I remember speaking one time when I used some language from William James's *Varieties of Religious Experience,* and it fell on the meeting like a wet blanket. On the other hand, one young man gave this testimony: "I'm prayed up, praised up, packed up, and ready to go up." There was a ringing response of hallelujahs and amens.

Why did I stay there for five years? Because there is nothing so enslaving as a religion of fear.

It was at Central Holiness University that I met Annette Gourley. She was in my class, but I knew her only as an exceptionally capable student until we were both members of a delegation sent to a convention at another Iowa college. She was the most interesting person I had ever talked to. From then on, we dated as much as we possibly could, getting around the restrictions with "accidental" meetings both on and off campus.

I graduated from Central Holiness University in June, 1914, not as well prepared to face the problems of life as I had been when I had completed DeSoto High School five years earlier. Though I had no clear idea of what I wanted to do in life, I thought I might like to be a college professor and teach sociology. The next year, I registered at the University of Wisconsin with my major in that field. I registered in the belief that Central Holiness University's unaccredited status would not work against my obtaining a master's degree. Although I made an excellent record in my work there, at the end of the year I was turned down for the master's degree because of the college I had attended. I was desperate. I had no more money for schooling, and I could not possibly get a teaching position without a master's degree. In my panic, I decided to go back to the work I thought I knew, farming. I decided to locate in Mississippi, where farmland was low in price.

I had been affected by the ferment of questions and new ideas at the University of Wisconsin, but I was still rigid and narrow and orthodox in my views. The real break for me came when I married Annette in 1915. She was a questioner and something of a rebel. She made me realize how many things I resented without being ready to admit it. Annette and I started out as rebels. We were rebels against the narrow-mindedness, fear, and intolerance that had been given us in the name of education.

However, although we could reject the intolerance of the school we had attended, we could not shake off the results of that education so easily. At the time, I did not realize my shortcomings. I thought that I was educated and competent. I little realized what five years of perverted education had done to me. I felt sure of success when we moved to that farm in Mississippi.

It was not a success. I was not good at handling my business. I was too much afraid of people to learn from my fellow farmers. When my father decided to sell his prosperous farm, uproot the family, come to Mississippi, and move on the same farm with us, I did not have the courage to tell him no.

It was a great mistake. Father took an immediate dislike for Annette and expressed it plainly. Under the circumstances, there was only one thing to do, and that was to tell Father I was going to leave.

I looked for a farm near Baton Rouge, Louisiana, and found one ten miles from the city. I was to discover that I had selected the place too hastily in a dry season. In normal years, it could not be drained well enough to raise a crop we could live on.

As a provider, I had proved thoroughly incompetent. We went through a long period of bleak poverty and want. Fortunately, Annette stood by me. She accepted a teaching job. I have sometimes thought she was just too stubborn to quit.

That was the situation when I learned of a vacancy in the Baton Rouge Post Office. That kind of work had never appealed to me, but I had a wife and baby to take care of with no income and no prospect of any.

I had a diploma saying I had completed a four-year college course, but my higher education began when I accepted the fact that it was essential for me to make a living. I applied for and got the post office job.

At the time I went to work at the post office, we were still living ten miles out of town, with dirt roads that in bad weather could become almost impassable. Annette wanted to simplify life. She quit teaching school and began talking of building a home close enough to the city for me to get to work more easily. In 1922, we moved to our newly built house in Wilson Place, on the corner of Florida and Laycock Streets. At the time, Florida Street was narrow and lightly graveled, only five blocks long, and separated from the city by a small pasture.

Wilson Place did not build up as rapidly as the promoters had hoped. For a long time, there were more vacant lots than houses. When we moved there, we brought part of our country life with us: our chickens, our cow, and our plan to make a garden. That was partly because we liked farm life and partly because we needed every bit of income we could get. We found a corner back of the garage where we could make a pen for the hens. The cow was picketted on vacant lots, wherever the grass was good. Our lot was rather small and did not have as much space as we wanted for a garden, so I made use of the vacant lot behind us. When the garden became established, we were able to sell its surplus.

Living in the suburbs, we missed our close contact with nature. When we had a little time free, we often went on a picnic in the nearby woods. You did not have to go far from the city then to find wild woodland. If we had an entire day, we might head for the hill country up around St. Francisville.

In 1929, we decided to buy a small place of our own in the country. We wanted our place to be on Highland Road, somewhere south of the university. We had to hunt for months, but finally we found twenty acres, six and a half miles south of the university, at a price we could afford. The property was on a hill above Highland Road–not a large hill, for it was only thirty or forty feet above Bayou Fountain, which runs alongside the road. It seemed rugged because the front of it was cut through by wooded ravines twenty feet deep.

After we bought the place, we did not try to make it pay a profit. It was a place where we could take the children and their friends for a summer picnic or for a winter campfire. It was a place where I could go for relaxation from the strains of the office by working out in the open or just walking around under the trees.

Bordering our property on one side was a small farm belonging to a black family who had owned their land for many years and were well respected in the community. I liked them and got along well with them, although we didn't always have exactly the same standards. During Prohibition days, they carried on a regular illegal liquor business. One day when I was out hiking with my daughter, I found their still, unattended but in operation, in the middle of a briar patch in the backwoods. I was a strong supporter of the Prohibition law, but I did not report them, because I also was acquainted with the city's richest bootlegger, who was operating his illegal liquor business in the largest hotel. I knew the enforcement officers knew all about it. If the rich white lawbreaker went unmolested, I didn't see why I should report the poor black farmer.

The family knew that I knew about their business. Before we built our house, they had moved into town, and the oldest son was managing the place as a hog and cattle farm. There were hogs next to us, lots of hogs. The young man fed them by collecting food scraps and slop from city hotels and restaurants, and he wasn't very careful or sanitary about his feeding. He did not have enough feed troughs, so much of the slop was poured out on the ground for the hogs to fight over. To say that the place stank is to state it mildly. Fortunately, the wind seldom blew from that direction.

On the opposite side and on the back, our little farm was bordered by the land of a wealthy white farmer who had formerly been a public school principal. Our relations with him were friendly, but we were never real friends. My respect for this man would have been greater if he had provided halfway decent housing for the families who worked for him. Two tenant houses were very close to us. I was called over one evening to help find a snake that had been seen in one of the houses. I did not find the snake, but I did see that there were so many holes in the walls that the snake could easily have gone out the way he came in.

That accounted for three sides of our place. In front, across Bayou Fountain, was the thousand-acre Longwood Plantation, but the residence on it was more than three miles away and on another road.

Florida Street had been a quiet place when we built there, a blind-end street reaching only two blocks west and three blocks east before it was cut off by pasture fences. Now the shrill honking of horns and loud screeching of brakes and tires filled our ears. Florida Street had become a four-lane concrete highway, the main entrance into the city, with a traffic count of fourteen thousand vehicles daily. We lived on the corner. The side street was also an important traffic artery leading to the city's industrial section. There was no traffic light at the corner and no sign to indicate who might have the right-of-way. Many times during the day and night, the right-of-way was disputed. There were wrecks and near-wrecks and loud arguments over who was to blame. We were tired of noise and tension. We wanted to get away. I was beginning to think of early retirement, and we could not retire on noisy Florida Street.

We decided the best plan would be to have a house built on our Highland Road property. We had done little to develop the farm, but after the federal rural electrification program brought electricity to the country, we had had a deep well drilled and put in an electric pump. Now the farm appeared to be the logical place. The university community was spreading in that direction. If we lived there, we could still be a part of the university life. Since 1937, when University, Louisiana, was made an independent post office, I had been working there because I preferred the university setting.

We wanted to build a nice house. When our home on Florida Street had been built twenty-five years earlier, we could pay for only the most economical construction. Now we were better off financially and could pay for what we wanted. We soon found, however, that something more than money was needed. This was in 1947, and wartime building restrictions were still in effect. We would have to get a permit from the Wartime Priority Board. We didn't worry about that. We mailed in our application and waited. It was turned down. Only returned World War II veterans would be given permits. Without the permit, we could not spend more than $400.

It looked impossible. I went down to the farm to think it over. I hiked about the woods until it occurred to me that I would do well to check over what there was on the place already which might be used in building a house.

Under a large live oak tree there was a storage house, fourteen by twenty feet, made of low-grade cypress. It had been a good place to keep tools and supplies, a shelter from a sudden rain, an adequate sleeping place for the few times I had stayed at the farm overnight, but not a place for us to live.

Then there was a pile of material from the old tenant house that I had torn down only a few months before. There was no question that house had been old. It had probably been a slave cabin before the Civil War. Everything about it was old, but there was good material in the pile. Nearly all the sills and the rafters were sound. The siding was of varying thicknesses and was rough and weather-worn, but it was all heart cypress and, such as it was, still usable. It might be possible to use the old galvanized roofing, too.

The longer I thought about our problem, the madder I got at the petty restrictions of wartime red tape. I drove home to suggest to Annette a plan of action. Suppose that we started with the building already under the live oak tree and added to it, using the material from the old tenant house. By spending $400 and doing the work ourselves, we could build a structure that we could live in until wartime permit restrictions were over. Then we would have a good house built.

Annette had not really wanted to leave the city, but she joined with me now in studying this plan from every angle. Finally, we decided to go ahead. That Saturday we started the job. Annette drew plans for the new house, and I began building. I don't know whether we would have tackled that job if we had known it would be almost as difficult to spend the $400 for supplies as it was to do the work of building. We soon found that regular hardware stores and lumberyards would sell us nothing without that wartime permit. I got some additional lumber from a new dealer, a returned veteran just starting a lumber business and glad to sell to anyone who came.

I couldn't hire a carpenter to help me, but finally found a student who knew something about building and could work on Saturdays. Nails were very scarce. The most we were ever able to buy at one time was ten pounds, and that was at a neighborhood grocery store. I had the same problems with electrical and plumbing supplies, and I often had to make do with substitutes. I was glad to think I was building only a temporary house.

At last the work on the house was far enough along that we could move in at any time. We put off moving because there was always a little more we wanted to get done. But one evening I came home from work to find that Annette had leased our Florida Street house as a shop. After that there was no question about it. The time had come to move to the farm. We borrowed a truck and moved to the house we had built.

That house was one we could live in, but it certainly offered nothing in the way of beauty. It was a square, boxlike building sitting on concrete-block piers, with a gable roof of secondhand galvanized iron made usable by soldering a multitude of nailholes. The house had been built with sheeting which consisted of a variety of old, rough, and very irregular lumber, so the whole had been covered with the only kind of siding we could buy, asphalt-roll siding with imitation red-brick finish. The effect could not be called attractive, but it certainly was striking. Inside, the appearance was somewhat better, but nothing was finished.

I had been so busy with the building that the grounds were completely neglected. There were weeds and briar patches between the house and the road.

Yet the farm was a beautiful place to live. The house sat on top of the hill surrounded by trees; a live oak arched over it. It was only six and a half miles to the university, so it was easy for me to get to work—except for the six months when we had no road.

Our new home was on a low-grade, narrow country road, one that sometimes flooded so that it was almost impassable. When a representative of the Louisiana Highway Commission called one morning to tell us that the road was to be widened and paved, we were delighted. When he asked us to donate the land needed to widen the road, we signed the papers promptly. In midsummer, a road contractor moved in and the work was started. The old road was torn up. Excavations were made for larger channels where bridges or culverts were needed. Pea gravel was hauled in and banked in a ridge along the roadway for miles. Then, in the late fall, the contractor was taken off our road so that he could build another that was politically more urgent.

We were almost marooned. All through that winter, we had no road. Highland Road toward Baton Rouge was completely out because the contractor had cut a deep channel across it for a bridge that had not been built. In order to get through with my car, I had to get out and study the stretches of mire until I knew them thoroughly and then hit them at a speed high enough for the car to slide over the mud without stopping. Then I would take a side road and go to my work at the University Post Office by a roundabout route.

That winter was a lonely time for Annette. We had no telephone, and nobody went past our house. I say no one; well, our neighbor who collected hotel scraps to feed his hogs went past in his old truck every other day, with a tractor hitched on in front to pull it through the mud. There was no one else. We were very thankful when the contractor finally came back to work in the spring and finished Highland Road. Shortly afterward the telephone company extended their line down the road, so we were able to have a telephone.

I retired from the post office in 1950. All our planning and work had been in preparation for early retirement, but when I finally left the University Post Office, I had a feeling of panic when I realized how much smaller my income would be. The buyer of our Florida Street property was not making his payments, and we had no idea how much time and litigation would be required to collect from him. For the present, my annuity was all we had to live on. I could see only one way to supplement it: We had land and a garden tractor. I would raise vegetables and try to sell them at a roadside stand in front of the house.

When spring came, I planted a big garden. The vegetables flourished, and we found that people stopped and bought at the self-service roadside stand. But neither Annette nor I liked it. It took too much work for the amount of money it brought in. Moreover, we found my annuity more adequate than I had expected. Before the second season ended, we quit the vegetable business. But we did learn two things from it we would find useful later: (1) people will come a long way for something they really want; (2) most people can be depended upon to be honest without being watched.

For every retired person, there are a few things necessary if retirement life is to be satisfactory. For me there were three requirements: (1) work that was challenging and worthwhile; (2) freedom to be myself; and (3) space.

In terms of work, my position in the Postal Service had been a good job, and I did well in it, but it did not call for constructive planning or for the best work I could do.

My need for freedom to be myself stemmed from my experience with a father who was a stern master and a religious fanatic. Afraid of my father and of his God, I was in complete subjection to my father's direction and to his authoritarian religion all the way through my college years in that narrow sectarian school. When I left my father's house and the intolerant religious group, that feeling of compulsion still followed me. I finally broke away from it, but then I began to resent any suggestion of authority. I wanted to choose the God whom I could worship, the political philosophy I could follow, the artists whose work I could admire, the music which could thrill me, and the work to which I could give myself.

The intensity of my need for space can only be explained by telling the story of a small boy. Perhaps I was five years old when I was wandering along the pasture fence by the road. Here a new box culvert had been installed under the road to carry the water from our pasture ditch. It was not very large, and it was built of new, clean lumber. I stooped down and looked through it. Then I thought, "I wonder if I can crawl through it and come out on the other side of the road." At this age, action follows thought promptly. It was fun to crawl into the culvert. It was just my size. I was about halfway through when I came to some framing which made it too narrow to pass. There was nothing to do but back up. It was cool weather, and I was wearing a coat. When I began to push backward, the coat bunched up around my back and held me tight. In an instant, I was seized by desperate panic. Here I was, stuck in a culvert in the middle of a dirt road, and nobody knew where I had gone. If I screamed, there was no one to hear me. Probably they couldn't hear me if they were right above me on the road.

I had a frightful vision of dying there and no one ever finding me. I struggled until I was exhausted. Then I began to think. I pushed my hands down and found that by working carefully, I could straighten out my coat so that it no longer bound me. Then I could slowly back my way out of the culvert. I was out, and I never crawled into another culvert. Forever after that, if I found myself in some closely restricted space, I would be gripped with some of that same panic. I wanted to be where I could see the world, could reach out in every direction, and could see the sky above me.

Our farm on the hill above Highland Road gave me space and freedom. Soon I would find the most interesting work I had ever attempted.

Both Annette and I grew up on family farms, where it was assumed that the land would produce all the fruit and vegetables the family needed. We expected our retirement farm to do that. I am not a first-class production farmer, because my curiosity has always been so great that I will try new crops when it might have been better to use the old standbys.

There is reason to look for new fruit varieties, for there are few that will thrive and bear in the warm, humid climate of south Louisiana. I found this out when I tried to grow my favorite plum, the blue damson. The damson trees thrived, becoming large and beautiful, but they never bloomed. We did not have a long enough winter for damson plums to bear fruit.

I cooperated with the Louisiana State University Experiment Station in testing some new fruit varieties which might be suited to our conditions. Most of them were of little value, but I did find some that were valuable additions to our orchard: the Baldwin pear; the Ribston apple; and three figs, the Florentine, the Hunt, and the green ischia.

When the seasons cooperate, we have more figs and pears and persimmons that we can use. Some of our ornamental trees, the mayhaw, crab apple, wild plum, and guava, produce fruit that is prized by jam and jelly makers, but we make little use of it, often giving the fruit to our friends.

As former farmers, we regarded our vegetable garden as even more necessary than the fruit trees. It was not a question of saving money by growing our own. We were particular about our vegetables. We insisted that they be fresh, and we had prejudices that had to be considered. For example, we liked the tender inner leaves of the Morris heading collards as boiled greens, but we had no use for the Georgia collards that are sold in grocery stores and grown in most southern gardens. I wouldn't touch okra, and neither of us was interested in ordinary cabbage, but we liked chard and Chinese cabbage. We liked carrots and sweet corn very much if they were fresh, but that meant not more than an hour's delay between the garden row and the cooking pot. We wanted a plentiful supply of red potatoes, but Annette would not think of using the grocery potatoes that had been stained with red dye to improve their color. Moreover, we wanted a steady supply of vegetables in late summer and winter, when grocery store stocks are at their poorest. So the vegetable garden was essential whether it was a profitable venture or not.

There is nothing that extends the value of the fruit orchard and the vegetable garden so much as a freezer. We bought a large chest freezer and have used it continuously. It holds pears and persimmons, figs and blackberries, and the juice from our satsuma oranges. We have frozen sweet corn, cauliflower, carrots, beets, beans, and many other things.

We have always been interested friends of wildlife, so we were thrilled one sunny morning to see a covey of quail walking sedately up the driveway, bobbing their heads and giving their covey call. And I was pleased to see rabbits start up as I walked across the pasture. We were less pleased with the rabbits the next winter, when we found our row of peas cut off close to the ground and half the carrot tops gone.

Wildlife was plentiful when we first came to the farm. We could always hear the bluebirds and meadowlarks singing, lined up on the pasture fenceposts.

Some animals, although numerous, were long a mystery to us. Soon after we moved into our house, we began to hear loud thumpings and scurryings in the attic. These sounded almost like a football match. I examined the attic repeatedly but never could see the intruders or find where they were getting in. The signs about the attic led me to think that they must be rodents of some sort. I set traps, but the beasts were not interested in any bait that I offered them.

I finally went to Dr. George Lowery, head of the Louisiana State University Zoological Museum, with my problem. He told me to try baiting the traps with a mixture of oatmeal and peanut butter. The first night I caught a large male wood rat, a beautiful specimen with a brown back, light gray belly, and very long tail, a species similar to the western pack rat. That specimen is now in the LSU Zoological Museum.

Wood rats are nocturnal and live in trees, so I then began to examine the trees near the house in the late evenings. There was a large live oak back of the house. From its largest branch hung an electric bulb, connected with the house by a wire running out from the attic. One night as it was getting dark I saw shadowy forms lined up along the wire, headed for the attic. The next day that wire came down; the attic was quiet once more.

We have always had a profusion of squirrels in our woods, mostly fox squirrels. Some people complain of the damage squirrels do, but we like them. We feed them regularly so they will come up and perform their antics before our picture window, where we can watch them.

The most beautiful and most intelligent of our wild animals is the raccoon. A raccoon can be a disaster in a patch of sweet corn when it is about right to use, and the raccoon knows just when it is ready. The coon's visit to the sweet corn would not be so bad if he would pull an ear and eat it clean. But he is a connoisseur, always looking for a better ear. He will rip the husks off one ear and take a bite and then break down a cornstalk to get another ear that is too high to reach, try it, and go on to another, perhaps a dozen ears in a single visit. It doesn't take many raccoons to clean out a home-garden patch of sweet corn.

One year I became so exasperated over their vandalism that I set steel traps along the corn rows. The raccoons were too smart for me until I tried bananas for bait. The next morning I found a raccoon, a beautiful animal, in the trap with his front leg crushed. As I approached, he looked at me. I stood and looked into those bright, intelligent eyes for a long time, and I understood why the Indians called the raccoon "little brother." I wished I could undo the trapping, but there was his mangled leg. The kindest thing I could do was to kill him quickly and painlessly. I have never set another trap for a raccoon.

Our love for wildlife did not extend to the poisonous snakes, which were numerous at first. We found moccasins, copperheads, rattlesnakes, and one coral snake. Along Bayou Fountain we used to see water moccasins lined up on the muddy bank one after another, sunning themselves. When Baton Rouge began to grow and the city encroached around us, the poisonous snakes were among the first wildlife to disappear.

Oil was discovered at the head of Bayou Fountain, and the stream began to flow with salt water and oilfield waste. First the fish disappeared, then the water moccasins. We have not seen a poisonous snake now for many years. We still have snakes, but they are blue runners, king snakes, and garter snakes, the quick-moving, friendly snakes that boys like to catch and try to make into pets.

Now the city has moved all around us, but we still have wild animals: the squirrels, occasional rabbits and opossums and skunks, and the recently arrived armadillos. The armadillos do their wandering at night, but we know they are here by the conical holes they leave when digging in the ground for insects.

Our little farm, with its open pasture and old trees, is a natural gathering place for birds. We can always see dozens of species without leaving the house. There are birds that are here all year, such as the cardinal, mockingbird, towhee, Carolina wren, brown thrasher, blue jay, titmouse, chickadee, and a variety of hawks, blackbirds, and woodpeckers. The barred owl talks to us at night from the tree outside the window.

In the winter, we have an added variety, the white-throated sparrows, the warblers, and sometimes the juncos and other birds from the Far North.

We have a special interest in hummingbirds and have kept feeders up for them in the summer. Sometimes they have come in numbers so great they cannot be counted. As residential subdivisions were built around us and neighbors copied our feeders, many of our hummingbirds were enticed away, but we still have our share of them.

We have some bird visitors that are of special interest because they are not often seen. One winter a spotted towhee from the Far West spent an entire season with us. He came to the feeder at such regular times each day that we could almost set our clocks by him. During two winters, our most striking visitor was a beautiful male Bullock's oriole, also from the West. Perhaps the most unusual visit was from two bald eagles who stopped for a time in one of our tallest red oaks before going on their way. As long as we have the woods, we will always have birds and animals.

One morning in spring, Annette and I were walking past an old redbud tree, under which dozens of little redbud seedlings were growing. Annette stopped to look at them, and then she said, "I wonder if you could move some of these little redbuds to the garden where they would grow better and then sell them next winter to people who might want redbuds."

She never did like to see anything wasted.

That was a simple problem, for I had a large garden plot worked up. But when I had the redbuds growing in the garden, I noticed small dogwoods crowded in my neighbor's pasture, and a few magnolias and tulip trees. At this very time I was studying Dr. Clair A. Brown's book *Trees and Shrubs of Louisiana* and trying to learn to identify all that I did not already know. I was particularly attracted to those trees and shrubs which he had listed as ornamental.

I had not thought of starting a nursery, but that was the beginning of one, a nursery specializing in native plants. I had been studying the native trees and shrubs of Louisiana. It would be necessary to make trips to forestland to find them. I soon formed a plan. I would have a nursery with native trees and shrubs for sale, and I would put good specimens of all of them in our woods so they would look as if they had always grown there.

In this way, a program was started that I would follow for the next twenty-five years. For the first year, the nursery plants were mostly the more familiar species, and most of our customers came because they expected to get what they wanted a little cheaper than elsewhere, and not because of an interest in native plants.

I was not satisfied. I was living and working with nature, but I found that I needed something more. The poet who wrote of "solitude" might well have said "nature" instead:

> How sweet, how passing sweet, is solitude!
> But grant me still a friend in my retreat,
> Whom I may whisper—solitude is sweet.

I was in love with nature and nature's plants, but I needed friends with whom I could share that love. Slowly, they came.

I increased the variety of my plants as I gradually learned where the rarer ones could be collected or how they could be propagated. Customers were surprised to find plants they had not expected. Then they might want to walk through our woods and talk about what they found there. The place slowly became known, not as a bargain center, but as a place to get good plants, and kinds that no other nursery carried.

There were other ways our story spread. One nearby garden club asked me to come to their meeting and discuss native ornamental plants. For this purpose, I took my camera and made up a set of colored slides to project on a screen. Then I was asked to speak at several other garden club meetings, and to make exhibits at flower shows in Baton Rouge and nearby places. All of this brought people who wanted to learn more about nature and the secret of growing things.

Some of the native shrubs were hard to propagate, especially the wild azalea. I always had to collect them from forestland, so I made many trips, often up into the hill country, and sometimes a hundred miles or more away.

At first I made all of these trips by myself. Then one day I was talking with Dr. George Lowery, and he asked me if his father might go with me on one of my collecting trips. His father enjoyed it very much and so did I. I began to invite other people, like my neighbor Dr. Shewen Slaughter, who was making a naturalistic planting of his own grounds. They all entered into the spirit of nature and added much to the pleasure of the trips.

I have always thought that the most outstanding flower, the most beautiful shrub, in the Louisiana forests is the wild azalea. So now I began a search for wild azaleas. It is possible to collect native plants more freely in Louisiana than in some other states because there is so much forestland. It is not difficult to get permission to collect plants from the undergrowth. Only the pine trees are sacred.

Whenever I had a free day, I headed off in search of wild azaleas. Much of that hunting was wasted time and travel. I know now that it is no use to look west across the Mississippi River, because wild azaleas do not grow on the Mississippi River flood plain. It is no use to drive south, because they do not grow on that flat coastal plain. But the trip south did bring results, for I saw pink flowers far back in a pasture and came home with young crab apples and wild plums.

I went southeast along the Amite River almost to its mouth at Lake Maurepas. I saw only one clump of wild azaleas, and they were on a ridge above the road at a bend in the river where it would have been a crime against the public to take them. But on my way back I found red honeysuckle. Livingston Parish is heavily wooded, so I began to cover every road, heading northward. I found a few azaleas here and there, but not in any great quantity.

I did find a number of native plants I wanted. The finest of them was the starbush, which grew in profusion along the Tickfaw River. The starbush is an evergreen bush in the magnolia family which has deep-red star-shaped flowers in early spring. I found out later that it was not respected in its local area but was called the "stinkbush" because of the aroma of its leaves.

This lack of respect for the starbush was brought out clearly on a trip to the Tickfaw to collect as many large starbushes as the car would hold. I was on a narrow country road. The ground was very wet. As I tried to park, the side of the road gave way and the car wheels sank down into the ditch. I tried every way but couldn't get the car out. I had a tow chain but no way to use it. I could only hope that someone would come along the road.

Meanwhile, I dug starbushes and placed them along the road to load later. After about an hour, a man came along in a pickup truck. He stopped, stared at my bushes, and blurted out, "What are you doing with those stinkbushes?" I explained that I was taking them over to Baton Rouge, where I could sell them. He looked a little longer, and then seemed satisfied. If I could sell "stinkbushes" and get real money for them, then I must not be crazy, whatever he thought of the people who bought them. He was then ready to pull my car back onto the firm road. I have always liked the fragrance of the starbush, and so have my customers.

When I finally found a dependable supply of wild azaleas, I was looking for another wild flowering shrub which seemed even more elusive. The Stewartia or wild camellia is a native shrub that has a beautiful flower about three inches across, with white-fringed petals and a purple center. It blooms in late spring and has a few flowers occasionally through the summer and early fall. It is rare because of its very exacting soil requirements.

I went to Clair Brown at LSU. He could not tell me exactly where to look but said that the plant did grow in Washington Parish, so I should be able to find it on the Louisiana State University forest reserve there. I consulted the foresters, who said they did not think that the Stewartia grew on the forest reserve. I now think they would not have known the Stewartia if they had walked through a thicket of it, but at the time, I accepted their opinion and did not look.

Finally I heard of a local woman who had found it in bloom. I called her up. "Yes," she said. "I found them." Then she told me precisely where they were. "Last Mother's Day, my two daughters wanted to celebrate the day by going on a picnic. We went up through Jackson, Louisiana, and across the bridge over Thompson Creek. There we took the road to the right. Seven miles up that road, we came to two bridges close together. We stopped by the first bridge, which was over a small creek that runs through a deep ravine. We climbed down to the water, took off our shoes, and waded up the stream. About three hundred feet from the road, we climbed up the bank on our right, and there the Stewartias were, in full bloom."

I followed her instructions exactly, except that I wore boots instead of going barefoot. This was during a wet period, and the banks were slippery. The sandbars beside the deep pools suggested quicksand. The nearly vertical bluff was too slick to climb until I found a ladder of scrub trees growing out from the bluff wall.

On the top were the Stewartias, just as I had been told. Stewartias were not the only interesting plants growing in those hills. I wanted oakleaf hydrangeas, and here were many of them on the edge of the bluff and along the banks of the gully. There were huckleberries, sparkleberries, witch hazel, and others. But the most valuable discovery was down along the stream bed itself. There, just about where the high water would reach in the rainy season, was an irregular row of little seedling plants, just right to set out in a nursery, and a large number of them were wild azaleas. There were no large bushes. Apparently the young plants were drowned out in floods and never grew up. Here among these streams in the hills was a place where I could get all the wild azaleas I needed.

Of all the trips I have made to forestland, near and far, I have special memories of one made to the Tunica Hills with my friend Julius Allen.

A hike through the Tunica Hills is a surprise to the newcomer because nothing he has seen from the road has prepared him for what he will find. The road curves along the top of the ridge with tall trees shutting both sides in, so it seems almost like a winding road across a tree-covered plain. The side road we took that day was arched over by trees and was narrow, barely wide enough for two cars to pass in dry weather. If the road were wet, it would be necessary for one car to stop while the other crept past. After a time, we found a place where we could pull over and park in a shallow ditch, leaving the road clear if another car should come along.

Then we climbed down the left bank into the woods. There we found ourselves in a dark trench or gully, shut in by tall trees and undergrowth and filled with ferns and other shade-loving plants. Obviously, it was an old road that had been in heavy use 150 years ago when all of this country that could be farmed was planted to cotton. The time came when cotton was no longer profitable, and most of this area went back to timber. Much later, the property owners began to raise cattle, and they needed roads once more to get around with their cars and trucks. Then, it was easier to make a new road, a little farther over on the ridge, and leave the old roadway to the trees with which nature had filled it.

We climbed over the far bank of the old roadway and looked down. The trees—oaks, elms, dogwoods, hickories, and ironwoods—towered high above our heads, but the ground fell away swiftly in a steep slope, far down to a sandy ditch with a tiny stream. Then we saw that the stream itself ran downhill sharply until we could not see the bottom. A great ravine opened up below us with tall trees arching out from the sides, making a canopy that the sun could not get through.

In spite of the continuous shade, the slopes were covered with rank undergrowth: oakleaf hydrangea, pawpaw, mountain hydrangea, young dogwoods, and, most of all, ferns of every description. The graceful marsh ferns were everywhere, and down by the stream were massive beds of Christmas ferns with dark green fronds more than three feet long. I had never seen such luxuriant Christmas ferns, or so many of them.

We climbed down, slipping or hanging onto small trees, to the ravine bottom 100 feet below. There the banks of the little stream were covered with a rich growth of moss and liverworts, together with the crown-shaped fronds of the northern maidenhair ferns, and others we could not name. It was the northern maidenhair ferns we were looking for, one of the most beautiful plants in nature.

I had a few of them in my home garden, and every fern lover who saw them wanted a share. Now I was seeking more of these lovely plants so I could share them with other lovers of nature at its finest. It was clear that the northern maidenhair likes shady places, for down in this ravine no sunlight ever penetrated the forest canopy during the summer.

We were in no hurry to leave. There was such exuberance of life, such unbelievable beauty, such an airy grace of growing things. We reveled in it. When at last we made our way up the slope, loaded with our collected plants, it seemed even steeper and more slippery than when going down. But there were young trees to grab and pull ourselves up, so we made our way to the top and across the old road to the car.

By this time my plant-growing project had become a small nursery, with a license from the Louisiana State Department of Agriculture and a sign beside the road. The sign read something like this:

Hilltop

Flowering Trees and Shrubs

of the Louisiana Woods

Emory Smith 11855 Highland Road

It was necessary to put prices on the plants displayed for sale, and that proved to be a problem. A nursery which buys its plants simply adds a percentage to the wholesale price, but I grew all of mine. To get some light on pricing, I visited local nurseries to see what they asked for plants we all sold, such as redbud, dogwood, magnolia, and a few others. One nursery owner gave me this advice: "If I were selling what you are, I would find out what others would charge, and then I would add something more, because no one else has those plants."

I did not follow his suggestion, because I did not want to charge more than I would be willing to pay if I were the buyer. Moreover, I have always been glad to help the occasional customer trying hard to beautify his home grounds with very little money to spend.

One year I had so many redbud trees that I ran an advertisement in the daily paper offering them for one dollar each, about half the regular price. That brought new customers, but it also brought bargain hunters. By that I mean persons who found that two-dollar trees could be bought for one dollar, and then immediately suggested that they should get two of them for a dollar and a half, or who looked over the dollar trees and then asked for a larger one that I had left in the row for sale at a higher price. I did not want that kind of customer. I quit advertising.

I did have special prices for children. This started with Dorothy. She was a little girl who lived just over the fence and was one of my closest friends. Dorothy loved violets. She didn't have much money to spend, so I let her have some potted violets for five cents each. Dorothy proved to be a good advertiser. Her small friends were soon coming over with her for potted violets. Five cents became the accepted price for the youngest customers.

Children also came looking for plants to give Mamma for Mother's Day or Christmas or a birthday. I never offered them anything free. That would have lowered their self-respect. I helped my six-year-old customer select the plant carefully, and was paid for it in a businesslike way. The price might not have been the same as for an adult. I never expected to make a profit from the children. Their business was fun.

The charm of one small customer caused me to lose completely a valued native plant. I did not learn her name or where she lived. She was a little girl about five years old. She came with her father and mother, who were buying huckleberry plants. Meanwhile, the little girl discovered a small huckleberry bush. I had dug it a year earlier from an unusual patch of evergreen dwarf huckleberries under the edge of the pine woods at the Cutrer Tree Farm off Greensburg Road in St. Helena Parish. This dainty plant was almost a foot tall and was covered with tiny bluegreen leaves and pink flowers. Here was a plant like Mamma was getting, but much more colorful, and just the right size for her. She wanted it.

I have usually refused to sell a plant when it was the only one of its kind, but in this case I thought, "She wants it so much. I can get some more, for I will be going back to the Cutrer Tree Farm soon." I finally told the parents they might buy it.

Back at the tree farm, I found that a woods fire had destroyed the entire patch of dwarf huckleberries. They did not sprout again, and I never found them anywhere else. But remembering the pride and happiness of that little girl as she carried the tiny plant in her arms to the car, I could not regret the sale.

Sometimes a nursery sale has just been the taking of a few minutes to wait on a cash customer. But often it has been much more than that. There is something about the love of native plants that makes a fraternity of all such enthusiasts. Customers I had never met came as friends, regardless of wealth, education, or social position. We found that we had much to share. We looked over the grounds and compared experiences before we got around to selecting the plant wanted that day. Sometimes a customer would stop again, if passing nearby, just to share a little more time with another lover of native plants.

The plant business could hardly be called a commercial nursery, but it had grown to the point where it added substantially to our retirement income. It was primarily my project, but Annette was enthusiastic about it all, except for one thing. Customers might come at any time, early in the morning or late in the evening, and I always made them welcome. What was worse, they might come at mealtime. No cook, when she has worked to prepare a good dinner, likes to wait and see it grow cold because a customer wants to talk about how to grow wild crab apples.

Annette told me her troubles, so I worked out this sign and put it beside the parking space:

LOOKING FOR PLANTS? SERVE YOURSELF.
PUT THE MONEY IN THE BOX BY THE GARAGE DOOR.
PLEASE DO NOT CALL US OUT ON BUSINESS
BETWEEN 12:00 AND 2:00 P.M. OR AFTER 5 O'CLOCK

That sign solved the problem. If anyone came while we were eating lunch, we simply ignored him and let him wait on himself. The customers seemed pleased with the plan also.

Those trips to forestlands to collect plants were not just for the nursery. On every trip I was looking for larger plants to set out in our woods, scattered about irregularly as though nature had planted them. This had gone on until there was some color and beauty to catch the eye at any time of the year from the opening of the huckleberry flowers about the first of January, followed soon by the spice bush, through the riot of spring bloom from the mayhaw, wild plum, swamp maple, wild azalea, and a dozen others, followed by magnolia, Stewartia, and Gordonia, and finishing the year with the late-autumn foliage of the oakleaf hydrangea in deep red and purple.

There were some special plants of outstanding beauty, such as the orange-flowered wild azalea, austrinum, and the bigleaf magnolia with its large white flowers and thirty-inch-long leaves.

It was good, but I was not satisfied. The forest with its beauty, grandeur, and mystery has always stirred my deepest feelings. I wanted to express those feelings in such a way that other people could share them with me. True art is a way of expressing the deepest feelings. It may be done in a painting, as when Landseer showed the thrill he felt in *A Stag at Bay*. It may be done in poetry, as in Wordsworth's "Daffodils," in which we feel the poet's excitement over the golden flowers fluttering in the breeze by the lake.

I wanted to express my feelings of the spirit of the forest by means of trees and shrubs, and on our own grounds. I never thought of making a park, because the forest is not neat, regular, or formal. I needed a plan for the grounds that would make all of this more accessible and more expressive, but I did not know how to go about making one.

One night I went to a lecture at the university sponsored by the School of Landscape Architecture. I do not remember a thing the speaker said, because just as he began, he threw upon the screen the ground plan of an old European cathedral. It had a great central hall or nave, and from that, in every direction, ran hallways leading to other rooms and on to others, with niches and passageways of every description. I seized upon it. This became my plan.

The nave and the other rooms were the open grassy plots; the walls were trees and shrubs and bamboo; the pillars were old tree trunks. There were paths leading in every direction to invite the visitor on to green openings, to unusual trees, to masses of beautiful flowers, or to where an unexpected opening before a half-concealed ravine revealed bright green ferns arching out from the bank while all beyond them remained a mystery. In short, the plan was an invitation to stop for a little while and marvel at nature's beauty.

Visitors came to walk over our paths. There were already many who knew about the native plants on our grounds. There were the ladies of the garden clubs who had often asked me to help them with their monthly programs and their garden shows. There were also many people from the university. They came because of a seed sown long ago. A few years before I retired, the university had started a course in landscape design and had engaged a young graduate of Cornell University, Dr. Robert S. Reich, to set up the course and head the department. I met Dr. Reich almost as soon as he reached the campus, and we became close friends.

After we moved to the farm, he visited us frequently. He was always "Bob" to us. It is an interesting fact that although he was here often and appreciated what we were trying to do on the place, he never offered any advice or gave any suggestion as to the design of the grounds. We did ask one of his advanced students, Roger Thompson, to help us on a specific problem, but the plan for the grounds was our own.

After we had been adding native flowering trees and shrubs to our woods for some time, Dr. Reich asked if he might bring his university classes to study the plants and learn of their use. I was glad to agree. I told him I might join him at times, but if I were busy, I would go my way and ignore them. Classes have been using our grounds for their field study ever since. That first class was small, but now they are so large they have to come in sections.

Persons on the university staff began to bring out guests from other states or even other countries to show them distinctive Louisiana trees and shrubs. They all came on scientific errands, not affected by the design of the grounds.

Others saw Hilltop differently. Students who had studied here as a part of the class often came back with family or special friends to show them a place with unusual appeal. Former students who had been away for years came back to wander over the little woodland they had loved. On Sunday afternoons young couples would come and spend hours among the trees. We felt sure they were courting, not doing classwork.

The neighborhood children, their friends, and their dogs have always loved our paths, our trees and grassy areas, the ups and downs of the terrain, and the hidden spots. They like to wander through the ravines where adults would not think of walking. Children find something here that they do not have in their own backyards or on the street or in public playgrounds.

We have always made them welcome, and they usually cooperate by not picking the flowers or damaging the plants or being too noisy near the house. To satisfy their curiosity, we have put the names of many of the trees on the trunks.

The children from the nearby residential subdivisions have never failed to call on us at Halloween. They cut across the shortest way, which means a long walk through the dark woods, a greater thrill than any treat they might get. We never give candy for a treat, but pecans, oranges, and kumquats from our own trees, with a few red apples from the store for brighter color. One year one of the mothers brought a group of children in a car around by the road, but that spoiled the fun of walking through the spooky dark woods. The car transportation has never been repeated.

There are many children, and most of them we do not know by name. We sometimes feel they take it for granted that they can use our place as a playground. But sometimes something happens to tell us this is not the case.

Some time ago I went into a little jewelry store near the university to have an adjustment made to my watch. The young man in charge greeted me. "You are Mr. Smith, aren't you?" When I said, "Yes," he went on, "I used to spend a lot of my time on your place. I really enjoyed playing there." He refused to let me pay for his work.

Then there was the boy who lived very close by. I had met him over here many times. He was killed in a tragic accident in his own home. The bereaved mother called up a few days after his death and asked if she might come over and see the places her boy had loved so much. She said he had spent much of his time on our grounds and had loved it more than any other place. I invited her to come. I walked with her over the grounds to show her the beautiful spots and also the features that appeal only to small boys, the hiding places under the bamboo bushes and the mud slides down the ravine banks. In some way it seemed to take some of the weight from her shoulders, and she went away comforted.

I am thankful for all the people who have told us what our woods have meant to them because I wanted to make this something more than a beautiful landscape design. I wanted to make those pathways tell something of the story of what life has taught me. To begin with, that is self-confidence and courage. It is to appreciate nature with its beauty and wonder and mystery and to know ourselves as the guardians of nature for the future. It is the love of people, all kinds of people, and the certainty they are what makes life worthwhile.

The woods now have a message for every season of the year. It is a cold, foggy day in midwinter, and the clouds are low in the gloomy morning. The dark strands of moss drooping from the trees suggest the hopelessness of Dante's *Inferno*. Then suddenly, from a nearby dogwood tree, a Carolina wren bursts forth into loud song. It seems to be saying, "Don't lose hope. The sun will shine tomorrow."

Tomorrow, the sun is shining. It lights up the brown leaves all over the ground. It gleams from the flaky bark of the red oak tree. It sparkles in the green tops of the pines. It may still be winter, but all is bright today, and the mottled green trillium plants are beginning to show among the dead leaves.

Then come with me in the spring, when the wild azalea is in full bloom. The starbush is crimson. The dogwoods and silverbells are covered with white. Under the trees, the ground is a carpet of violets and trillium. All the earth is rejoicing.

Yes, and the woods can speak to us when a hurricane is roaring through, when the supple birch trees lie flat on the ground, and the great oaks bend and rock in the wind. If I venture out upon the path, I must brace myself with all my strength to stand against the wind, and I watch fearfully lest one of the tall trees go over in the blast. Tomorrow, the oaks will stand there majestically, and they seem to be saying to us, "The violence of the storm only made us stronger."

I have hoped that those who follow these paths find the strength and confidence and security that has come to me from walking with nature. I have learned that I must find life's truth, life's purpose, and its mission in that part of the world close to me.

My experience with my Father and his God did not drive me away from church membership. Annette and I have always been active church members. When we first came to Louisiana, there was only one church we could attend conveniently, the Jones Creek Baptist Church, so we went there, taking part in all church activites.

When we moved into Baton Rouge, there were two Methodist churches to choose from. We joined the smaller one, Keener Memorial Methodist Church, and liked it except for one thing. The Ku Klux Klan had too much influence in it. At that time, right after World War I, the Klan became very strong around Baton Rouge.

We transferred our membership to First Methodist Church and were active members there until a controversy arose over the Methodist students at Louisiana State University. On campus, the Methodist Students had an organization called the Wesley Foundation, with a director appointed by the Methodist Conference. The Wesley Foundation was under the control of the nearest Methodist church; in this case, First Methodist.

In the school year 1940–1941, the students were demanding the right to manage their own program at the student center and to have religious services there on Sunday so that it would not be necessary to go three miles to church. Feelings became very hot. Finally the First Church pastor announced decisively that there would be no change in the student center.

I was angry because I regarded that as religious tyranny. There was only one way to get around it, and that was to start a new church at the university. Consequently, when Lynn Case, the students' champion and a professor of history at LSU, asked me if I thought we could start a University Methodist Church, I told him I was ready to join him in the attempt. The new church was organized on September 8, 1941. During World War II, we met in the University Theatre, finally moving into our own building at the edge of campus in May, 1951.

Although church membership has meant a great deal to me, I can get a greater uplift of spirit when I see the sun gild the tops of the oak trees with a crown of glory or watch a band of laughing children playing under those trees. I know that it is a privilege to help my neighbor find calmness of mind and uplift of spirit by contributing to an environment that speaks of peace and joy. So we have worked and planned to enhance the beauty of our bit of nature. To me, planning this woodland has been more than a landscape job. It has been an attempt to put into tangible form my philosophy of life.

The faith that I have found cannot be expressed by any of the creeds recited in the churches. I cannot join in any of them without great reservations. A faith is better expressed by the life we share with other people than by formal words.

If I were to try to write the creed by which I live, it would be something like this:

I believe in the natural world about me and its fitness as a home for the human family. It is my responsibility to do all I can to preserve this world of nature, to prevent its destruction or defilement.

I believe in the people among whom I live. All of them have faults, but so do I. It is in the people about us that we find our strength and the joy of life's fulfillment.

I believe in myself, that I can meet life's problems with courage and strength and calmness.

I believe in the world of nature in all that it means: the trees and the flowers about me, the smallest division of the molecule and the most distant stars of the universe. As long as I live, I wish to face that world with insistent curiosity, but also with reverence and wonder. I wish to be a good custodian. May the small part of nature under my control be the better because of the way in which I have used it.

Mexican plum
Prunus mexicana

Dedication
of
Hilltop Arboretum

The public dedication of Hilltop Arboretum, Louisiana State University, took place on March 28, 1982. Emory Smith gave the following address as part of the ceremony.

I am sure that there are people who wonder why I would give away this valuable property. Let me try to tell you. Landscape classes have been coming out here for many years to study our native plants and their use in landscape design. I have been honored to have a part in their work of making our environment a better place in which to live. I want to be able to look to the future and know that I can still have a part in that, even when I am no longer here in person. That is one reason for the donation, but not the greatest.

I have always loved the woods. I have loved the beauty, the mystery, the wonder, and the surprises that I found there. I well remember one day, as a small boy in Iowa, when I went across the road to a small wooded pasture. I thought then that those bur oaks were big trees, though I know now that they were not. It was the time of year when the crab apples in front of the oaks were covered with pink blossoms. Then, down under those trees, among the dead leaves, I found a marvelous display of snow-white trillium, together with trout lilies and violets.

Later, when I had grown up and come south, I was living in the hills of Mississippi where there were beech and tulip trees 150 feet tall, with trunks more than 5 feet in diameter. One day, as I was walking through those woods, I came upon the first wild azalea I had even seen in bloom. That fairy-like flower is one of the loveliest things nature has ever produced. I could scarcely believe such beauty was possible.

So, in my southern home, I wanted to know nature with all its beauty, its mystery and wonder, and I wanted to make the most of it here on my own grounds. I also wanted to share it with all who came my way.

I ran the Hilltop Nursery in order to share native plants with other people. At the same time, I planted trees and shrubs from Louisiana forests in our own woods so that they would look as though they belonged there. To do this, it was necessary to study forestlands in order to learn what was there.

I have gone to the woods all over Livingston and St. Helena Parishes. I have tramped through the Tunica Hills and along the Middle Fork of Thompson Creek. I have climbed over the steep hills north of Woodville, Mississippi, and have explored Pushpatappa Creek in Washington Parish.

I wanted to bring the finest specimens that could be taken from these woods back to my place. I have only halfway succeeded. That is another of the reasons I am donating Hilltop to the University and to my community. I have not been able to do it myself. I need your help to finish the job, and to make this the arboretum it should be.

There is yet another reason for wanting to make the most of nature here, and it is a very personal one. As a boy, I was trained to believe in a religion of intolerance and fear. I learned to think of God as an implacable judge who would have no mercy on anyone who did not conform exactly to His rules. I did not think I measured up very well, so I was afraid. I was always afraid. When a storm came up on a summer night, with the thunder crashing and the wind roaring through the maple trees, I would lie awake trembling. To me, it seemed to be the sound of Judgment Day, and I would never be able to pass the test.

There was one place where I could get away from that tension and fear. It was when I went to the woods and gave myself up to nature. In the back wooded pasture, the oak, the elm, and the hickory trees were standing firm and open to the sky. Underneath these were hazel bushes and many wildflowers. The place was alive with the songs of the birds and the chatter of the striped chipmunk squirrels. There, in the woods, my strain and my fears would vanish, and I would find a world I could trust and in which I could feel secure. It was more than an escape. It was a sanctuary. I wanted to make my woods here a sanctuary where anyone whose load has become too heavy might walk its paths and feel the healing touch of nature. May it always be open to anyone who needs that healing touch.

This arboretum is yours. It is yours to enjoy, and yours to help complete.

Japanese persimmon
Diospyros kaki

Appendix

Emory Smith's Favorite Plants

The following list of Emory Smith's favorite plants is from Dr. Robert Reich, professor emeritus, LSU School of Landscape Architecture.

1. Bigleaf magnolia (*Magnolia macrophylla*)—large white flowers surrounded by large leaves
2. Oakleaf hydrangea (*Hydrangea quercifolia*)—large panicles of white flowers in late spring, turning pinkish then brown; attractive pink flower buds
3. Wild azalea (*Rhododendron canescens*)—pink to white flowers, conspicuous and very fragrant before and after foliage; attractive pink flower buds
4. Cherokee rose (*Rosa laevigata*)—beautiful, fragrant white flowers in spring, red fruit in fall and winter; glossy evergreen foliage
5. Mexican plum (*Prunus mexicana*)—pale pink flowers, early spring, fragrant
6. Red buckeye (*Aesculus pavia*)—panicles of bright red flowers in early spring, after the foliage but above it

7. Spice bush (*Lindera benzoin*)—tiny, fragrant yellow green flowers in spring, before the foliage; yellow autumn color; aromatic
8. Japanese persimmon (*Diospyros kaki*)—large orange fruit, Emory's favorite; Mrs. Smith used to make a bread/cake with the persimmons
9. Pignut hickory (*Carya glabra*)—bright yellow autumn color
10. Silverbell (*Halesia diptera*)—white, bell-shaped flowers in spring about the time foliage comes; interesting canopy as flowers hang down and sunlight shines through the foliage
11. Stewartia (*Stewartia malacodendron*)—camellia-like flowers; hard to find
12. Trillium spp.—surprise appearance in spring with purple brown flowers above mottled foliage
13. May apple (*Podophyllum peltatum*)—surprise appearance in early spring with bright green foliage, white flowers and yellow fruit nodding under the foliage
14. Flame azalea (*Rhododendron austrinum*)—yellow orange flowers, very fragrant

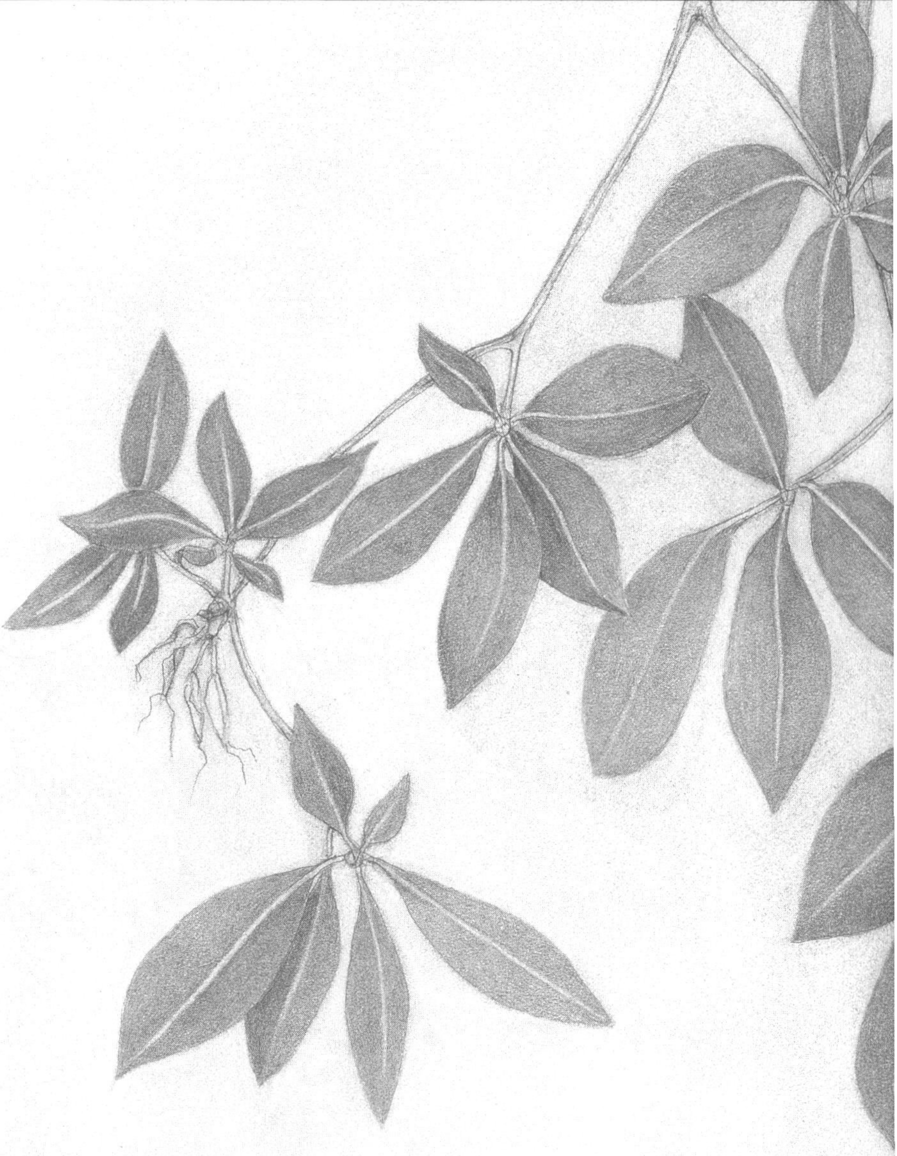